shadows drag untidy

Adrian Flavell

shadows drag untidy

Acknowledgements

Poems included in this collection have been previously published
in the following:
*The Australian, Beyond the Rainbow, Burley, Egg Poetry,
NSW School Magazine, Patterns, Polestar Writers Journal,
Positive Words, Regime, Social Alternatives* and *Tamba.*

To my family, friends and dogs
with love and thanks

for the light
for the shadow

and the space between

shadows drag untidy
ISBN 978 1 76041 842 7
Copyright © text Adrian Flavell 2020
Cover photo: Johanna Flavell

First published 2020 by
GINNINDERRA PRESS
PO Box 3461 Port Adelaide 5015
www.ginninderrapress.com.au

Contents

shadows drag untidy	9
on removing a tattoo	11
for Emily	12
broken	13
the scream of years	14
scared blind	16
that was enough	18
wedding vows	19
mistaking love…	20
everyone was losing	22
her face	23
the bridge	24
the escape	25
their story is tangled	26
not yet at rest	28
a lovescape in 3 parts	30
careless	31
in celebration	32
fish wit	33
ice queen	34
so they sat	35
while outside	37
loose change	38
casual	39
these dogs	40
the old bloke and his bush dogs	41
obedience	43
terror	44
a management issue	45
the dingo	46

the kangaroo hunt or a ute, 2 cartons and 3 dogs	47
at camp: near the old dam	48
sunrise	49
the meeting	50
a sort of redemption	51
the dark	52
black sorrow	53
seeking refuge	54
the campsite	55
five memories of travel	56
river gum: a story of drought	58
end of day	59
a postcard moment	60
pickers: grape harvest	61
sleeping out	62
despite the weather	63
sightseeing	64
at the beach	65
winter coast – a tidal romance	67
like a child	68
desperate	69
the sea	70
across the bay	71
a fishing trip	72
fishing boats	73
Sydney Harbour	74
the complexity of seagull	75
poker face	76
a cinematic accident	77
the passing of season	78
Normandy – a veteran's view	79
something in the ritual	80

the eulogy	81
the estate clearance	82
the burial	83
ancestral forensics	84
urgent hands	85
the missing	86
case notes	88
the petrol station	90
hotel heroics	91
closing time (1)	92
final drinks	93
closing time (2)	94
city scene	95
umbrellas	96
Friday p.m.	97
the almost artist	98
the opening of an exhibition	99
global warming / peer pressure	100
chess	101
by the Torrens	102
homeless	103
for Nick	105
Leonard Cohen: a tribute in 3 parts	106
the goat as sacrifice	107
the market stall	108
desert wolf – a brief history of the Middle East	109
intervention	111
emergency department	112
a view from Virgin	113
red geraniums	114
out of season	115
poppies	116

summer apples	117
sweet pickings	118
catholic soccer – holy indulgence	119
pelicans	120
ducks	121
free range / takeaway	122
dog	123
the German Shepherd	124

shadows drag untidy

the past
is shadow

that stretches

close hanging the light

never too far

untidy dragging

raking through
as memory
to track and trail

those lost moments
balanced in tension

hair-trigger romantics

keeping it together
for things to conceal

with things unstuck

blurring the fine line delicate

but no longer
a safe ground

so treading a water
running back
to out-tide

no soft-shoe shuffle
to unzip
like ripened fruit

just darkening clouds
as echo of mood

and the spider crawl
of shadows
upon ceiling

that shifts the silence
from not listening

to just watch

on removing a tattoo

1 – at the clinic:

>as if
>by removing the tattoo
>she could erase the past
>
>start afresh / again /
>with a clean slate
>
>worth a try
>
>even if skin deep

2 – d.i.y.:

>he tried
>peeling the skin
>
>as his dad
>taught him
>
>when fishing for leatherjacket

for Emily

daylight collapsed

and now

it's her sunset
that burns itself
deep into horizon

here

open to the
wind of pain
and the creep
of strangled grief

she stays
with those she knew

and the sad-eyed memories

that do not pass so easy

but still howl
into the wreckage
of life on edge

broken

1

    he broke (down)

    like a horse

    unable to take
    the final jump

2

    she broke (down)

    like a car

    overheating
    to make it
    up the freeway

the scream of years

needing to find out
what he knew to be true

he took to talking

discussing

throwing out life secrets
like used tissues

catching memories
and hurling them full length

into explanations

of where and how

yes and but

nothing so easy

few too simple

out of touch
over the edge

dealing from
his pack of lies

he flipped hands
of guilt and blame

slipped from the truth
with the ease
of changing channel

clutching at
the image of straw

he coaxed responses
in a fumble of promise

and sought to stifle
the scream of years

scared blind

unseen

not seeing

scared blind
by knowing you're right

and now

too close to fact
too near the event

you're witness
to a different time

where bridges are burnt

stables bolted
and hearts locked too late

the milk has spilt

spread already
to cover lost ground

no time out

the one – too – many
of the camel's back
has brought you to this

crumple – shocked
love – stunned

thinking the bizarre
and living the mediocre

you've been
to where they think
you're going

seen over the wall
through the fence

ran the distance
with the audience
one step ahead

clapping / jeering / throwing
wolves amongst the babies

and knowing you'd arrive
in time
to catch them in the act

that was enough

watching for something

when there's
nothing to recognise

but somewhere
that fear

of withered years

without anything to say
about being forever

for that shadow falls

and falls again

and whatever is left
is enough
to touch a life
and define a loneliness

unlike that

of laughter and luck
and not much thought

but then
at times

that was enough

wedding vows

the window
broke like a promise

and shattered trust

to every corner
of their lives

mistaking love…

all together too soon
the action froze

catching you resting
on the off-beat
of another's life

you didn't get away

stayed there

stood their staring

facing the music

back to the wall
folding into shadow

then picking up pieces
of people
fallen from love

all the king's horses
and his men
left them

so why bother

except to be caught
with your fingers
slippery in honey

licking the tips

tipping the lives
of others
who fell to pieces

mistaking love
for a nursery rhyme

everyone was losing

everyone was losing

> – lost bets
> – lost beliefs
> – lost car keys/jobs/sleep

lost track of when and where

(and time was misplaced

and couldn't be made up)

some lost

> – their love
> – their loves
> – their looks
> – their limbs
> – their temper/appetite/memory/hair

so finally
in a world of gesture
it was accepted

that loss
was an amputation

performed without anaesthetic

her face

her face
the mirror of all nights

the blackness
of all endings

that silent life
which leaves tears
full – feeling

no need to ask

for he has spent hours
in mourning

brought against this
the separation and partings

of unhappiness

of forgetting the rules
that put him
out of the game

and she searches
in random

to settle who's to blame

the bridge

his is the face
of ruined stillness

with lines drawn
somewhere beyond misery

he who

for too long
had to disguise
the collaboration
of cruelty and memory

now stands

above the menace

beyond the routine
urgency of panic

his eyes set
somewhere behind the sun

and the agony
of a single tear
cuts through

to snatch
at some eloquence

for this departure

the escape

the night
wears through

as moon's wash
spills the length of highway

headlights gaze
without blinking

billboards flick dreams

stations change their music
to a currency of doubt

nightmares cut loose
to plague the narrow margin
between chaos
and the wound

for the forgotten things
left locked

whose meaning
is still unfolding
as asphalt chases away

and each kilometre engages
an invisible disturbance

where escape
is more than
not being there

their story is tangled

their story is tangled
in a balance

that leaves families
to shake loose
and select a version

on the rim
of other things

that could be said

that could be heard

but she chooses
to wake in a night

where half-dark moon
breathes dampness
through trees

and windows frost
to the stranger's touch

and she prefers
to leave
lost dreams shredded

hanging ragged
in another life

while he drives
a fugitive past
expecting to collide

with that
first glare of sun

not yet at rest

my eyes as watchdog
through the dynasty
of lives gone astray

bitch growling mouth
snapping at the legacy
of misplaced loves

my face changed
and charged
with lack of sleep

when the gasping
and scrape for air
mirrored the struggle
that gave me life

that grip and tear
of family flesh
peels me back

>	I am the seal
>	on arctic flows
>
>	the stain on linen ice
>
>	the shattered skull
>	tipping the treacle brain

so taste my blood

plum redness

crimson

through the shriek of love

suck the acid kiss
of a dying mother

and drag mourners
up the steps of memory

to steady the fear

not yet at rest

a lovescape in 3 parts

part 1 – each lovescape
is a journal
of profit and loss

writtenonbodies
that disregard
the could-be-of-disaster

part 2 – to be without you
is the waiting
for moons to spin
and settle dangerous
on waves
to other worlds

the darkness
of lives unknown
in seas swirling restless

part 3 – you burn

against the fire
of my mood

your scorched cheeks
turn in soundless breath

I leave marks
on those I love

careless

she fumbles through love

like a kid

careless on the road

in celebration

smell the urgency of skin

>   the mood of blood
>   the chaos of pain

and celebrate

the agony of single tear

fish wit

you fillet me
with your blade of wit

I'm cut from the bone

exposing the humour
of compromised flesh

and the tragedy
of dysfunctional organs

ice queen

the avalanche of my affection
slid you snowbound

into love's envelope

and sealed you
with a lick

that melted
a gallery of frost

so they sat

clouds lifted

like a shrug
of indifference

so they sat

until the hills
became black

and light sucked
into a darkness
beyond their back

but lending / bending
to a forecast

where the sorrow
in her eyes
yielded a depth

that overlapped
the soft-edged outline
of unfinished echo

they chose

and in that choice

they pushed
out of shape

a sadness
of invisible wounding

and in there

somewhere

the answer moved
gentle beside them

while outside

doors slam unseen
in anger / pain / shame

the arch and jerk
of domestic spasm

while outside

a parrot hits the window
in fear of glazed flight

it shudders…

like nodding heads
of daisies and dreamers

and the waves

that never reach shore

loose change

his advice
hits the pavement
like loose change

fetched up
with car keys

casual

casual
in her lies

she spread them
like peanut paste

with anaphylactic intent

these dogs

the night settles
to its darkness

as the cry
of a wild dog

lost dog / dumped dog /

no longer a puppy dog

these dogs

sweeping town boundaries
in spreading circles
of crazy web
and frantic prowl

they howl

and your mind
jerks clear

free to scout the pack

and for a moment

you pace a fence line

in assumption
of a place to fit

where just to be
is the death of isolation

the old bloke and his bush dogs

the dogs came
as a pack
of social nature

not solitary
in their searchings

with eyes
penetrating the darkness
of the shack

the dogs came
because he hadn't

no bites
or snarling here

shoulders close – contact
pushing the doorway

they moved
through the room
to sniff old plates
at the table

and nudge bowls
reckless
edging the sink

these creatures prowl
in a howl of hunger

and more

in search
of movement or scent
known and trusted

but little is left

old boots
and a jacket
tossed careless
across the bed

are slim pickings
for old friends

obedience

the dog sits
edging the roadside

back legs folded
the length of gutter

as though
waiting for a bus

it is still there
at night

with a turd
beside its blanket

by morning

it's just skid marks
and only
a passing flurry

as the dog
coughs for air

desperate to catch at life

as it bleeds
the edging of roadside

terror

from somewhere

the scream of rabbit

snatched by jaws

......of dog
......of trap

so that split moment
before scream

was the complete silence

of terror

a management issue

dingoes

pack-drifting the park

sniff over
weekend campsites

selecting and sampling
leftover careless meals

but then

they stiffen

taste the air

ears prick
to the stretch of early morning

a chase of scent

a blink of motion

other decisions had been made

the dingo

the loneliness of dingo

for that moment
isolated and still

silhouette in spotlight

she is alone
at the point of death

suspended briefly
between hunt and hunted

between breath and blood

and her scream
echoes the valley

blasting its darkness
beyond any dreaming

and then

the arrogance of fence

as her body
is hung through wire

in this final act of displacement

the kangaroo hunt
or
a ute, 2 cartons and 3 dogs

silhouette chase
at sunset
had come to this

and knowing
it had lost

the kangaroo
turned its head

one ear
already hanging jagged
like a snapped branch

               – at what point
               did it choose
               to accept the jaws

               and not judge
               the menace of teeth

               to catch a final breath
               and fold to landscape?

they could have shot

but left it
for the ripping of dog

at camp: near the old dam

shadows drag untidy
along the bank
like a rough draft

barbed wire
scars the eastern end
with catches of hair
fluttering in some
corruption of victory

crows hack
like smokers
dislodging phlegm

somewhere
a solitary barking
inhabits the valley

a single duck
splits the dam
and wedges
apart the evening

smoke filters
the early drizzle
as we drift
in the growing coldness

sunrise

the day ahead
stretches to a yawn

like a puppy

fresh from napping

the meeting

light licks
through the night

as the smile
of dawn

grins

into fragile friendship

a sort of redemption

the day
draws you out

there's an invitation
to a ritual tasting
of early sun

and late regrets

for things not forgotten

but in those shadow-lands
of forfeit and sorrow

there's still room

for a morning
that leans gently

the dark

I felt the dark

clouds northern this sky
to a sorrow

making it elsewhere

black sorrow

night is reluctant

slow to leave
this morning

like the crow

picking over feathers
of its flattened mate

seeking refuge

rosellas
in the autumn oak

harlequin fruit

rainbow splashes
amidst a foreign forest

the campsite

rising smoke
rubs between trees

edging towards canopy

in a seductive roll

five memories of travel

1

        wild ducks
        shelter beside the silo

        too hot
        to chase the trailings of wheat

2

        chainsaws growl
        along the roadside

        making wider

        a track
        already leading nowhere

3

        fish slip the creek

        like shadows
        chasing yesterday

4

        startled geese
        fly toward the mountain

        carrying sunset
        in funeral entourage

5

    at edge of day
    earth gentle slides
    into a darkness

river gum: a story of drought

river gum

its roots
grasp at creek bank

as though
wringing out
the last drop

from winter's wash

end of day

the sun

grazes shadow
to just a whisper

so that trees
weep solemn light
in their stillness

as pigeons
fly low
in wing-tip squadron

a postcard moment

sunset had been
a postcard moment

a choreography
of cloud and crimson

reckless and confident
in its glory

pickers: grape harvest

decanting
the last evening vintage

so drops
at end of day

splash

the aching dark

to stain
the silence

while

in the softness of distance

a wasting fire
flicks silhouettes
of tribal animation

as people eat
and rest
a long day's picking

sleeping out

all night
under the threat of fog

the bodies set
like a cheap ring
in the echo of fire

share spaces
that others have filled

and with morning

footprints
carelessly scattered
in the cold light
of a colder beach

reveal a blind search

for all that's gone missing

despite the weather

the sky
closed over
like a wound

inward wrapping
and warping
into a broken night
of cracked vision
and lyrical chaos

even so…

a full moon!

so complete
in search
of words

and the dignity
of new sound

while we
cough and shiver
in celebration
of lunar concert

and find joy
in the welcome

of another greeting

sightseeing

the sea spits
the length of beach

its mouth foaming
like a poisoned dog

the wind snarling
a rabid jaw
to rip and tear

the pack encircles
to howl and hunt

from the bus
it is clear

there is little welcome

in this bite of coast

at the beach

the wind has left

gone now
in a final tearing

the sea flattens
to a shallow breathing

geometry of wharf
dissects the sky

the beach settles
into afternoon

people are forgotten

people forget

their talk surrenders
to the passing tide

floating words
that are careless
in the current

and leave memories
drifting without meaning

as dramatic shadows
of things
that were once

and the sea
tips and licks
cheers and jeers

in a coastal carnival
that leaves seagulls
to chorus their discontent

winter coast – a tidal romance

early winter
draws tighter its days

as we sit
folded against the wind
raking the beach
for things to say

fingers drag
through memories

hands smooth the unspoken

but the night deepens
as a chasing tide

with you

kicking through darkness
like waves at land's end

like a child

the sea

calm for this
time of year

licks the beach

like a child
wanting her ice cream
to last beyond the moment

desperate

the waves claw

grab at the shoreline

in effort
to crawl further
from tidal pull

while seagulls
drift the breeze

wilful in submission

the sea

1

    the sea pulls back
    to the depth
    of its breath

    like the slow turn
    of clothes slipped

    and left hanging
    naked in silhouette

2

    the sea
    empties its stomach

    and old tidemarks
    spill across sand

    while driftwood
    hesitates to leave

    like the drunk
    reluctant at closing time

across the bay

a fisherman
cleans the catch

while his dog
clouds the sky
with seagulls

in shallows
pelicans yawn
in expectation

there is little afternoon left
as light falls to shadow

and mountains set
across the bay

within the whisper of storm

a fishing trip

near the jetty

seagulls
cheat and deal
over discarded bait

while dogs
negotiate their inheritance

after the barbecue

fishing boats

in the yawning
of each dawn

fishing boats

are spat out

by tide
and the orchestra

of overdraft
and diminishing returns

Sydney Harbour

yachts litter
the harbour

as first world scatterings

of discarded bonus

the complexity of seagull

1

    seagulls
    as coastal security

    patrol the sand

    in checking
    for tidal leftover

    and the refuse
    of foreign fortune

2

    seagulls
    at Bondi

    standing yoga

    meditating
    the chip

    and the repetition
    of wave

poker face

aces tumbled

tripped from the pack
with unspoken luck

in a hand
that couldn't be beaten

and that
being the case

he chucked the glass

choosing to split a nose
rather than the deck

a cinematic accident

at the river bend

the bank is wrinkled
like an old man's elbow

and tyre tracks
crease the road edge

while beyond

just out of sight

an upturned bike

with one wheel
cliché – circling
cinematically

and somewhere else

not far

a dragging through spinifex

the passing of season

he hung there
as a xmas decoration

missed

in the rush
to celebrate new year

while summer slipped away
like a terminal patient

with relatives too busy

to celebrate
the passing of season

but what had died
within memory

cannot recall

the filter
of edge and borders

things to cross

have been

left unspoken
for too long

and now hoped
to be forgiven

Normandy – a veteran's view

my father
walks his garden

now grown beyond
the tended years
of his concern

while early pigeons squabble
in fruitless repetition
of habit

and he tells me

for the first time

that the smell
of a dead bird
returns him to Normandy

and unable to answer
I fold into his shadow

now edging
a sunset
of last chance

something in the ritual

we gathered around

to hear his breath rasp
into the greater silence

and when he died

there was a feeling
of one less person
in the room

and in that vacuum
was a suction
of loss and memory

and needing
to run wild beaches
in the scream of storm

the eulogy

he paused at the comma

(maybe) for too long

but in that time
he saw the need
to edit his own life
and sort the first draft

for twists of truth and fantasy

and morphine trails of fiction

yet still to snatch
at some eloquence

for this
and his own departure

while the grieving of family

moved restless
on the printed page

the estate clearance

we sought a meaning
from his belongings

sifted the litter
of his years

the dusted combings
of eccentricity

but with clues rare

we came short
of all that was

and now would be

the burial

I have stood
by too many graves

like putting shoes
back into a box

whether they fit
…or not

the pinch and tuck
or the smallness of form

ancestral forensics

in our family tree

there are branches
where people swing

and should you dig

the roots
will unbury the dead

urgent hands

urgent hands spread
their lies of love
and unclip and clasp

behind the door
around the wall

soft open mouth
dropping guard
against the kindness
of her friend

and thin excuses
for visits
lasting too long

become the tyranny
that inhabits
the darkness of thought

the missing

1

    the hand turned

    a half-twist

    as though to wave
    the royal wave

    as gesture
    for the crowd

    a token of contact

    but no

    instead

    just wrist-deep
    in mud packed too hard
    for more than a tortured twist

    fingers curling
    in final slow spasm

    this shallow grave
    is almost lost
    in the layering
    of mangrove tide

2

>she said
>she may be late
>
>they remember that
>(and other things)
>
>as the shadows shuffle
>
>in the shelter of pain
>
>and the night
>will forever
>
>just be black

3

>and with time
>
>they will find
>more bones
>at this land's edge
>
>the sea
>is a careless
>curator of the dead

case notes

the signs were there
           (almost neon)

the jagged talk of family

the broken toys and joys

the dog's collar
still chained
to the fence

but for her

the theatre of unhinged life
became the alibi of silence

slipping further out of reach
in the routine of shadows

so that now

she locks the toilet door
and crumples to the bowl

she smells him there

the paper gagging
to be flushed

his shit smearing the porcelain
like roadkill spread
the length of highway

she curses this life

and this room
with its one rusting lock

the petrol station

when petrol spills
to rainbow
under his car

a life shifts to crazy image

of: a fist through glass
       a razor surfing wrists
       a fork in the tongue
       a cattle truck of stars

with his heart
running on empty

in the ruined sequence
of a shattered journey

hotel heroics

she leans brave
for a midday drinker

hotel warrior

Boudicca of bar

knocking back
and topping up

eyes levelling the shot

finger skimming the rim

swigging
till the purse surrenders
or the card
can take no more

then

with the truckie's jacket
wrapped around
as white flag

she follows him outside

to retreat behind enemy lines

closing time (1)

the pub
echoes the chant

of one
for the road

in the theatre
of last resort

while outside

the froth and bubble
of a beer-headed boy

spills out

like an upturned keg

final drinks

the landscape
leans into horizon

as a lone drinker

propping the bar
for final drinks

closing time (2)

bodies poured
into the street

like whiskey
smooth easing the edge

in a casual run-off

from the push and shove
of lives
careless lived

in daily chaos

city scene

summer

when skirts
flip and kick

a city scene

their legs

keen to catch a sun

between the office
and the coffee

umbrellas

from above

a rainy city street

is an outburst
of mushrooms

Friday p.m.

people spread
the length of street

like butter toast

wiped with a knife

                *

students pour
from the bus

like spilt paint

as uniforms colour
the texture of street

the almost artist

he painted
on Saturdays

but mixed colours

with the anxiety
of a working week

the opening of an exhibition

then a crowd
of grey to black

swilled through

like mourners
in search
of a lost coffin

global warming / peer pressure

oceans squeeze
the land

like a boy

set to pop his face

before a date

chess

just for a moment
the family of magpies
playing the back lawn

became a board
of black and white

until checkmate

by neighbour's cat

by the Torrens

the image of a dead swan
sits darkly
along this river bank

its black silence
echoing a deeper quiet
of torture in the night

for such a city
for such a sight

its throat cut
like watermelon
with fish spitting
its last seeds of life

while joggers
parade in whispers
and no voice
beyond a murmur
to consecrate
what once was sacred

homeless

it's raining

the bus shelter is already taken

like an airport
with flights cancelled
and passengers
settling next to luggage

but here

a shadowed figure
with his life
stacked in a shopping trolley

has claimed territory /
marked its borders

she moves away
from what she can see
to a place unseen

and wraps the tarp
around her world
to a blue cocoon

it's raining

her clothes are fused
in dampness of misery

she drifts the edge of sleep
within shadows of danger

but pulls back

she knows the darkness
as messenger of threat

it's still raining

she's cold and alone

the wind bites
and stabs through
the sadness of shelter

inside she cries
for lost mothers / daughters

and folds in the bitterness

not caring any more
for the unknown / for the possible

for the impossible

for Nick

some days
have been our days

but the year
has passed

flicked through a calendar

like us

for that time
to catch up

Leonard Cohen: a tribute in 3 parts

1

flagging a failed reprieve

the possum is executed
on the power line

bearing witness
to an incineration
of freedom's flight

2

above the road

two sets of trophy sneakers

sad drooping
like puppies
bagged and dumped

in a drowning
of lost dreams

3

but the bird
on this wire

is an echo of hope

seeking forgiveness
wherever it is given

the goat as sacrifice

almost biblical
in proportion
of scenes cast

yet within
mythical to misery

the goat screamed

        – they do that –

no quiet transition to death

but like your child

they scream
with each
slash or stab

and in the thickness
that is the smell of blood

its eyes
will read of panic

and mirror our fears
of edging/falling
towards death

the market stall

the pig's head
looked almost
smug

a half-sneer
in the knowledge
of something

not known
in its slaughter

or just
the final scream

softened
by the butcher's
practised hand

to somehow banish
the baked image
of his firstborn

desert wolf – a brief history of the Middle East

you…

wolf of memory

howling up visions

of desperate days
in final hours

of bodies
flung and torn

and you howl
to call in the pack

to chew on carcass
still breathing
but bleeding

into the rubble
of desert night

as moon rises

and rises again

to still shifting sand
that doesn't wait

in bringing rage
and the grief
in those dead

to those
still dying

and feeding predators

as history
crouches and pounces

wherever

there is prey

intervention

in other cities

that smell of burning
is bread

not family

emergency department

nurses here
school like baitfish

each splash
a focus frenzy

within the threat

that is
the chaos of carnage

a view from Virgin

arthritic river twisting
for a softer bed
through mountain veins

while clouds
wrap the mountains

as welcome gifts
for first rain

red geraniums

outside

the silent rain
darkens the dirt

settling the dust
to the fashion
of tame shadow

inside

the flower vase
spits red geraniums

as blood clots
on the mantelpiece

out of season

the rain
is soft

a gentle soak
out of season

a reminder
of drifting dreams

not sure
where to be

but here

now

it's welcome

and fragile colours
shadow its quest
to make sense

of all things
that have been chosen

or not

in this

the first cry
of a summer's dawn

poppies

poppies
opening
as we watch

speaking softly

expecting to hear
the crack
of petal

summer apples

the apples are gone

between the rosellas
and unseasonal wind

they've been resettled
as a tattered carpet
through the stretch of orchard

yet still

an occasional one
left in the tree

but baked
like gourmet dessert

sweet pickings

now
the size of an orange

the moon

is solitary
in its orchard of stars

waiting
to be picked

catholic soccer – holy indulgence

the nuns
have a habit

they can't kick

not properly

unless they hitch
and tuck
and somehow not reveal

except in confession

to atone
for the sin
of their own goals

pelicans

pelicans

like wind-scattered
sheets of music

settle into the breeze

as they lift
and drift

in their own
orchestra of flight

ducks

ducklings
spill across the road

like water

escaping a burst pipe

*

ducks gather
as dance troupe

in careless tumble

towards the dam

free range / takeaway

finally
the early hint of setting

as the sun stretches
to an orange sky

and I watch chickens

one less now

because of a life choice
(made on their behalf)

free range – takeaway

her feathers
whispering / floating
like an early mist

then to find the body

a stump of russet brown

her head chewed neatly
to a guillotine precision
of crimson cartilage

and now buried

others scratch
above her rotting

regardless of
the reign of terror

dog

(for Luka)

our German Shepherd
in the pub

the guinness
of the canine world

*

his barking
litters the sky
with galahs

pink and grey
screams of indignation

*

our dog
amongst the wallabies

the ultimate in fast food

the German Shepherd

(for Luka and me)

kneeling by the bed
to stroke the slow breathing
of a dying dog

feeling a history
that shared nine years
of doing things together

except this

he's dying alone
(I'm just there
or here
or wherever)

he's the first

head butting the door
(as he does / did)

to force entry

and to drag his tongue
across my face

for the last time

to leave this
and every world

that we share
and could know

between the shadow
and the light

www.ingramcontent.com/pod-product-compliance
Lightning Source LLC
Chambersburg PA
CBHW070919080526
44589CB00013B/1360